RICHARD THONGER

A CALENDAR
OF GERMAN
CUSTOMS

RICHARD THONGER

A CALENDAR
OF GERMAN
CUSTOMS

OSWALD WOLFF

LONDON

© OSWALD WOLFF (PUBLISHERS) LTD 1966

BASED ON
VOLKSBRAUCH IM JAHRESLAUF
BY HEDI LEHMANN
(ERNST HEIMERAN VERLAG, MUNICH)

DESIGNED BY ELWYN BLACKER

Blocks for illustrations by courtesy of
DEUTSCHE HOFFMANN–LA ROCHE AG

MADE AND PRINTED IN GREAT BRITAIN
BY THE GARDEN CITY PRESS LIMITED
LETCHWORTH, HERTFORDSHIRE

Contents

9

Foreword

As an Englishman born not very far from Stonehenge and taught by a Cornish nurse to turn his pockets inside out in case of pixies, to bow to a new moon and never to put new shoes on a table, I first went to Germany nineteen years ago, in the years of rubble and ragged shoes, and made German friends who taught me how to tell fortunes on New Year's Eve by pouring lead into water, and clubbed together to buy me a reliable horoscope. From them I learned to look at the calendar, and now Miss Hedi Lehmann has been kind enough to let me re-house the charming pictures from her book in a text of my own. Some of the details, especially the eye-witness account of the Passion Play at Oberammergau, the story of the tame roebuck under Hunting Customs, and some of the Carnival material, are mine, but most of the facts I owe to Miss Lehmann's patient research.

This book aims at a selection of customs practised on German territory and overflows into Belgium, Northern France, Switzerland, Austria and Sweden.

R.T.

Hampstead, March 1965

Lordling's favour, April showers,
Lady's love and blooming flowers,
Luck at cards and luck at dice
Change, don't doubt it, in a trice.

Herren Gunst und Aprillenwetter,
Frauenlieb und Rosenblätter,
Würfel- und auch Kartenspiel,
Wenden sich, wer's glauben will.

Rejoicing Day

Lätare

WINTER has ruled us hard and long, but Summer is on the march, and as the two giants skirmish we mime their battle with robust partiality and cheer the champion of warm sun and green fields. In the ancient city of Augsburg, wrote one citizen, 'on this day do they play a game in all parts of the land wherein the young boys do carry plaited bread (*Bretzeln*) on long sticks about the town and two men play Summer and Winter, he who plays Summer has

evergreen or ivy upon him and Winter is masked and terrible. And these two fight. And Summer wins and strikes Winter down.'

Rejoicing Day, the fourth Sunday in Lent, is called *Lätare* in Germany from the opening word in Latin of chapter 66, verse 10 of the Book of the Prophet Isaiah: 'Rejoice ye with Jerusalem, and be glad with her, all that love her: rejoice for joy with her, all that mourn for her.'

So Rejoicing Day was given a name and took its place in the Christian calendar, but the dancers and mummers and marchers were after sunshine rather than sanctity.

In Eastern districts of Germany they used to give Winter a funeral and called it 'Carrying Death away' (*Todaustragen*). To a song about 'the scythe-smith' Death and our hopes of life from Christ's resurrection, the Riesengebirge inhabitants would carry a straw doll to the 'death stone' and then burn it or drown it. People would scatter in fear, since Death was supposed to be hovering in wait for the last one away. Sombre notions attached to the straw doll: people would pay the bearers money not to let the 'Death' look into their windows. Tiring eventually of this death-play, Germans took more and more to rituals of welcome to Summer instead.

The 'Summer Victory of Eisenach' (*Eisenacher Sommergewinn*) went on for centuries, a splendid procession which assembled and moved off at noon. A crowd of children marched along, dressed as Easter bunnies, song-birds, cockchafers, frogs and butterflies. They held 'spring sticks' (*Frühlingsstäbe*) in their hands and sang:

> Now we have driven Death out
> And brought the dear Summer again,
> Had we not driven him out,
> This year long would he remain.

> *Nun han den Tod wir ausgetrieben*
> *und bringen den lieben Sommer wieder,*
> *hätten wir den Tod nicht ausgetrieben,*
> *so wär er dies Jahr wohl hinne blieben.*

16

Two great carts drove along in the children's midst. Winter stood on his cart straddling seven-league legs and crowned with a shock of white hair, but he was no match for Mistress Sunshine and her escort of garlanded children. Up at the front rode the mascot for the day, the sign of a crowing cock.

In Heidelberg it is the Summer's Day procession, and the children come in hundreds carrying their Summer's Day sticks (*Sommertagsstecken*). The hazel wands are sprigged with violets and hung with eggs, apples and pretzels.

Many songs are known for Summer's Day, and they are ancient; one was well established in Rhodes as early as 200 B.C. Breslau children used to sing Summer's Day songs as they walked from place to place, carrying their decorated sticks, which they called *Schmackoster*, 'Easter nibbles'.

Winter and Summer in the Steiermark are teams of young men. The Winter men put on fur jackets and advance, armed with bakers' shovels, flails and reels of twine, to meet the Summer men with their sickles, scythes and pitchforks. And in Appenzell in Switzerland Winter and Summer argue, and slap each other loudly on the shoulder.

Over to the West, a Flemish tradition in Brabant has it that 'the Earl of half-way through Lent', the *sinte Greef*, rides his horse across the roofs by night. Children dream of the Greef on his milk-white steed, with his servant by his side, and put out little baskets: when they wake up, the Earl has put sweets in them. Girls old enough to be interested in boys wait eagerly for Greefs made of gingerbread or marzipan. The more you get, the more young men are supposed to be after you, but look out – if you've been sulky or fickle, you may get a Greef made of brown bread or pottery.

As the summer evenings crept on, the Swiss housewife would put away her candles, and at Islikon they still say good-bye to the candle-light by 'sending it downstream'. The candles are lighted at dusk inside a small tower made of sticks and coloured paper, set on a wooden raft and decorated with banners bearing moons and stars as signs of darkness. Couples are dancing on a floor near the water's edge as the little boat is pushed out to stream: sud-

17

denly the music stops, everyone rushes to the rail, and the cry of '*Füürio, de Bach brönnt!*' – 'Fury – O, the brook's afire – O' speeds the candle-light on its long way down the Rhine to the North Sea.

And a Thuringian variation, where the spring 'looks out of the water': the Mühlhausen schoolchildren used to walk to the Popperöder Brunnen: the girls wore wreaths of flowers on their heads, and all carried flower-sprigged 'summer sticks' in their hands; at the end of their walk they sank their sticks and wreaths in the spring, and made a flower-bed under the blue water.

The Salvator Season

Salvator-Saison

BAVARIA does not actually claim to have invented beer, but does state without apparent fear of contradiction that the Paulaner Brewery cellar becomes the true centre of the beer-drinking world once the *Salvator-Quelle*, the Salvator Spring, which is on the Nockherberg in the Müncher Au, begins to flow shortly before St. Joseph's Day, 19th March. Salvator beer has been flowing since 1651: it was first named 'Holy Father Beer' or '*Sankt Vater-Bier*', and popular speech soon corrupted the word to Salvator. Monks of the order of St. Francis of Paula would honour his name-day by handing out a special beer, which, it is recorded, 'excelled all other', and the occasion on which this beer was drawn became a fair. Popular as it was, the court would attend it with pomp, ceremony and regularity, and today for Munich the spring only begins with the Salvator season. Guests of honour led by the Bavarian State Government taste the first

barrel during the morning, and the general pilgrimage to the Salvator premises begins at 2 o'clock; the premises are vast, holding ten thousand souls in the hall and in the garden.

Other names for great beer came along: *Triumphator, Maximator, Animator*. Beer and Munich were firmly linked, and if you were one of the 37,840 inhabitants of the Bavarian capital in 1784 you could reckon on the services of 52 brewers and 144 proprietors of licensed premises identified by handsome wrought-iron signs. There in old Munich you 'went to a cellar', and drank your beer and argued, or just drank, elbows on the heavy scrubbed table, pewter pot or wooden mug in your fist. Then the 'beer bell' sounded, and you began to count your small change, for if you were drinking outside the city walls you had to pay a gate fine for coming in after closing time: 4.30 in winter, 8.30 in summer, one kreuzer for yourself and two for your horse. But that was only until 10 o'clock; after the 'great closing' only one gate would let you back into Munich, and the gate fine was expensive – six kreuzers for man or horse, dog or donkey.

Some drinking-places in Bavaria would put up *Rausch-Tafeln*,

naming 26 different degrees of intoxication and the price you would have to pay to achieve it, from 39 kreuzers to 2 guilders 42 kreuzers. The learned Lichtenberg, in his *Mythologie der Deutschen*, notes 111 High German terms for degrees of drunkenness, but only 56 in Low German. This wealth of nicknames did not distract the Germans from a proper attitude to the beer itself. You drank it where it was drawn, at 8 to 10 degrees Centigrade, and it was tested for strength by accredited inspectors, worthy and respected men who appeared in teams of up to three at a time, dressed for the job in leather breeches. A few jugs of today's beer were poured over a wooden bench. The inspectors planked their leather seats down on the wet wood and sat stiffly drinking for an hour by the glass. Then they rose as one man, and if the beer was up to strength, the bench stuck fast to their breeches and rose with them. If it did not, the beer was 'too light', and the brewer had to pay a fine.

The inventor of beer eludes accurate identification. It may well have been Gambrinus, King of Brabant at the time of Charlemagne; or, as the Egyptians claim, the God Osiris. Brewers do not worry, and poets flourish on the spirit and morality of drinking. Sebastian Brant wrote in his *Narrenschiff*, the 'Vessel of Fools', in 1494:

> Much must the fool drink and deeply,
> While the wise man drinketh moderately,
> And doth more good unto his health
> Than he who tips barrels into himself.

> *Ein Narr muoss vil gsoffen han,*
> *Eyn Wyser maesslich trinken kan,*
> *Und ist gesünder vil damit,*
> *Dann der mit Kübeln in sich schütt.*

And a rhyme from Alsace claims world citizenship for beer-drinking:

> Sure I forget all my trouble and sorrow
> When I drink beer, a good pot of beer,
> Nor do I bother to think of tomorrow –
> The world doth it cheer, my good pot of beer.

> *Vergesse tut mer Müej un Sorge,*
> *bim e Schöppel Bier!*
> *Mer denkt nit an den andern Morge,*
> *s'ischt e Weltplaisir!*

Courting

Liebe

THE YOUNG MEN of Dux in the Sudetenland used to chew a
sort of gum and leave the end hanging out between their teeth
as they danced. The girl would be invited to bite the end off, and
if she did, she was hooked; if not, the young man could look elsewhere, for

> If thou likest not my chew,
> There's no love for me and you.

> *Magst du nit mei Mummla,*
> *So hast du mi nit lieb.*

They were simpler about it in the Eifel. The lad would put a
bottle of wine on the table between him and his young lady, and
if she fetched two glasses, she was willing. The Rhinelander was
even more direct, merely banging on his girl's bedroom door: if
she did not speak, there was nothing doing.

In the Alps, love of climbing and the serenading tradition took
the form of 'windowing', called *'Fensterln'* in Bavaria and
'Kiltgang' in Switzerland. Alpine farmhouses are large, girls sleep
in the top bedroom, and the wall offers no footholds, so the
young man takes a ladder with him and having gained the
heights of his beloved's window-ledge, 'stands there half the
night through with icicles on his nose'. The immediate purpose
of the climb was conversation, sometimes formalised into
rhymed questions, and answers indicating yes or no. A general
notion that 'windowing' was hallowed custom and that if one
stuck it out, one might get a leg over the window-sill, competed
with ecclesiastical disapproval. It was a sport, with rules; rich
boys who took hired hands with them to cover their rearguard

were looked down on, and in some places there was a close season: no 'windowing' on Tuesdays, Thursdays, Saturdays or Sundays. And although society tolerated the same ladder frequently at the same window, the line was drawn at young men 'like squirrels with seven nests' or at girls 'whose windows looked like dovecotes'.

Other courting customs were public and formal. Young men in the Rhineland, the Eifel, the Saar and Brunswick used to bid for girls at the 'May fee', the *Mailehen*, generally held on May Day, when the name of every girl of courting age was called out. Any lad could bid for any girl, and once she was knocked down to him, he became her dancing-partner either for the month of May or for the whole year. A girl might not like her partner, and in Münstereifel she would show her displeasure by giving him flowers picked from a broad-bean stalk. In the Siebengebirge near Bonn, the lads would go to a copse on a hill the night after the auction, and there sing the words of an old song and burn 'their last year's May-girl' in the shape of a straw dolly. Lastly they would pick a green branch and plant it in front of their new May-girl's front door.

All this was very orderly, but exceptions were provided for: catch-phrases to warn a rival away from one's girl, and 'hat-lifting' (*Hutlüften*) for a young man courting a girl away from his own village: the local lads would lie in wait for him, seize his hat and only give it back in exchange for a nip of brandy all round.

Once a young man in the Alps was going steady, he could look forward to receiving seasonal presents from his sweetheart: red hard-boiled eggs at Easter, doughnuts for Kermesse (*Kirchweih*), and for Christmas a 'jest' (*Scherz*), the end cut off a cake called a *Kletzenbrot*. The gifts were wrapped in a white cloth, embroidered on its four corners with the girl's Christian name and a scrap of verse. Some of the verses are tender:

As much I love thee	*Ich lieb dich so fest*
As her branches the tree,	*Wie der Baum seine Äst,*
And the stars by the sky	*Wie der Himmel seine Stern.*
Are loved as you by I.	*Grad so hab ich dich gern.*

And others less so:

> My love for thee will never wobble,
> But if thou deceive me, go to the devil.

> *Dass ich dich lieb, ist ohne Zweifel,*
> *Wirst du mir untreu, hol dich der Teufel.*

Presents were not all: the young man could expect love-letters as well, and highly elaborated they were, beautifully decorated and folded into a fan shape which opened out into four, eight or even sixteen hearts filled with verses.

Betrothals

Verlobung

In OLDEN DAYS the Germans regarded the act of becoming engaged as a final contract, and up to the seventeenth century betrothed couples would live together as man and wife. A plain 'Will you marry me?' and the answer 'Yes' were not enough: there had to be a ceremony before witnesses. At one time the man had to give the woman a girdle, a book with silver clasps or two Imperial thalers, and received from her his wedding shirt, a hatband and an embroidered handkerchief called a *Näsedook*.

In Merovingian times, between the years 430 and 751, the young woman appeared with her betrothed before her assembled relatives and in-laws, beautifully dressed, with jewels in her hair. She stretched out her right hand to him and he took it, pressed it with love and filled it with money, kissed her on the lips and slipped the engagement ring on her finger. His present to her was a pair of elegantly embroidered slippers. This motif is found in the story of *Aschenputtel*, the German Cinderella – a golden slipper for a prince's bride – and the slippers were a symbol of the wife's subjection to the husband, so that if the traditional position is reversed, the German wife does not 'wear the breeches' but 'has her husband under her slipper'. The money was important: the young man was buying his bride from her father, sometimes with land, and in some districts even the name of the engagement ceremony was *Leihkauf* or *Lenkauf*, a transaction.

Bavarian girls used to celebrate their engagement by eating a *Ja-Schmarrn*, a kind of omelette, with their fiancé, and in Brunswick the young man had to write his beloved a long and handsome letter.

Trial engagements were often tolerated, especially, it is said, in

Swabia, but were beset by rules, for example on the island of Borkum, where an ordeal called *Beetnemen* was organised for young men who hesitated too long, or at least were still closeted with their young women after midnight. The local lads would surround the house, put a guard on every door and window, and send an emissary to bang on the door and invite surrender. If there was no reply, the seige was maintained all night to give the couple time to reconsider. At first light the seige party went into action: the chimney was stopped up to fill the house with smoke, the invaders tried all the doors and windows, and if they held, took a few tiles off the roof, climbed into the loft and searched the house for the *Bösewicht*, the villain. Once found, he had to answer the question 'Are you two engaged?' A 'Yes'

26

would produce congratulations and the public announcement of the happy event throughout the village, but if the young man could only manage a 'No' he was tethered to a rope and dragged three times through the nearest patch of water.

Engagements were generally celebrated the day before the first banns were read in church. In some districts, such as Anna-berg in Saxony, the couple had to go to church to hear the banns read, while not far away, at Crottendorf or Breitenbrunn, they were told to stay at home. Traditionally, German engaged couples did not have to wait long for their wedding: usually six to eight weeks, the time required for busy fingers to complete the trousseau.

The 'Six o'clock Strike' at Zürich

Sechseläuten

SPRING COMES to Zürich traditionally on the Monday after the vernal equinox, when the *Mareielis*, little girls in white frocks, crowd through the streets waving wreaths decorated with flowers and ribbons. The little boys wear coloured ribbons on their white shirts and masks and paper hats, and ring the door-bells as they go, calling out '*Urscheli, Batz, Batz*' for which they are given small presents. The older boys collect money for their straw doll, the spook or *Böögg*, which is burnt at the top of a tall pole when the clock strikes six. As English boys make a bonfire for Guy Fawkes, Zürich boys burn the ghost of winter.

The 'six o'clock strike', originally the occasion for craftsmen

to mark the end of the first day's work in summer (there were only two seasons for this purpose, summer and winter) blossomed out into a general celebration, and since 1819 a procession has marched through the streets, a score of guilds in traditional costume, first by torchlight at night but later by day: boatmen dressed as Venetian gondoliers, bakers carrying huge loaves, pork-butchers with great sausages on their shoulders, blacksmiths with outsize hammers, tinsmiths, doctors, surgeons. The winter spook, the *Böögg*, is still burnt on its long pole when the clock strikes six, and sometimes there is a splendid firework display down by the lake. To avoid bad weather, the date has been edged forward to the third Monday in April.

After the noisy *Aussenfeier* in the open air the guildsmen, who today are not all craftsmen, retire to their guild houses, eat a long and elaborate supper, pay each other visits and drink healths while they engage in lengthy verbal duels charged with ponderous wit.

Saints' Days in Spring
Namensfeste

As GERMANY became Christian, heathen custom was not abolished, but largely taken over by the Church. Sometimes heathen names were left, as the name Easter remains, from the goddess Ostara.

In the sunny South Tyrol St. Peter's Day, the 22nd February, was the first day for work in the vineyards, and in East Friesland the children used to take a *Binde-Brief*, a 'binding letter' to every man named Peter. The letter read:

Peter's Day has come around,
And Peter shall be bound.
Not with rope and not with bast,
But with this letter we bind him fast.

Heute ist Peters Tag,
da man Peter binden mag.
Wir binden ihn nicht mit Seil oder Bast,
sondern mit diesem Brieflein fast.

So Peter was bound, and had to buy himself free with pennies for cake or sweets. On the same day in Westphalia the children would oblige householders by banging on the doorposts with hammers and singing doggerel 'to drive out the vermin'.

St. Matthew is much loved in Western Germany, where Matthias was once very common both as a Christian name and as a surname, and is the only Apostle buried, at Trier, on German soil. Having been beheaded, he was adopted as the patron saint of pork-butchers (the axe being the mark of their profession) and swineherds, who called their Saint's day 'Tigges-Tag' and would celebrate it by dancing about, cracking whips and shouting 'Matheis bricht's Eis' (Matt-ice breaks the ice): Matthew would bring them the spring. St. Matthew's Day in Cologne was the occasion for sinister fortune-telling, when a bowl of water was put out overnight and an ivy leaf put into it for each member of the family; if any leaf was wet or blackened next morning, death was not far off.

In March there was hope of sunshine. 'Kunigund, macht warm von unt' was the doggerel prayer for warm weather to the saintly wife of the Emperor Henry II, buried in 1033 at the convent of Kaufungen, near Kassel, where we can admire the tomb devised by the great Tilman Riemenschneider.

On 12th March they used to say 'Gregori macht den Tag gleich der Nacht' (Gregory makes day like night), remembering how the vernal equinox had crept further and further back into winter (in the sixteenth century it was back to 12th March) before Pope Gregory XIII reformed the calendar.

March 17th:

| Gertrude and her mouse | Gertrud mit der Maus |
| Drive spinners out of house. | treibt die Spinnerinnen raus. |

Born a daughter of Pippin the Elder in the seventh century, St. Gertrude is often pictured in old German calendars holding a distaff with two mice running up it – mice allegedly sent by the Devil to tempt her to impatience. She protects households from mice and is the patroness of gardening, which good housewives should begin on St. Gertrude's Day. Travellers and seamen invoke her aid, and she provides the first night's lodging for departed souls on their way to purgatory (St. Michael being responsible for the second).

March 19th and St. Joseph, patron of family life and housing

matters. Silesian children used to put out little baskets on St. Joseph's Day, and the *Josefsgeklimper* would come and fill them with nice things to eat.

March 25th, and the swallows should be back for the long-established Feast of the Annunciation.

Finally St. George's Day on 23rd April, time to take the cattle to the high Alpine pastures. Children can run barefoot, and drinking water will do you no harm now: 'the poison goes into the frogs and snakes', as they say in the Iser hills. Boys in the Inn valley 'ring the pasture in' as they go from farm to farm in shorts and shirts with large and small bells hung about them. Look after the *Grasausläuter* and you will get good hay and a bumper crop.

Palm Sunday
Palmsonntag

PALM-TREES are hard to find in the North, but anything green or evergreen will do to celebrate the ride into Jerusalem: willow, hazel, birch, box, yew or holly. Near Basel they prefer holly with red berries, and in the Tyrol they peel the bark from a slim mast of hazel, paint it in red and blue spirals, tie it with sprigs of box and dress it up with silk ribbons, tinsel, pretzels and apples. In many places they make a *Gemeindepalm*, a 'parish palm', out of a fir or larch and stand it in the church.

The 'palm donkey' had his place of honour in the *Palmesel-prozession*. One kind was made of wood, with a carved figure of Christ on his back, and was carried through the village and round the church before the Easter service began. Sometimes one of the clergy would ride a real donkey, always at the tail end of the

33

3—ACOGC

procession: hence the name 'palm donkey' for some one who gets up late on Palm Sunday or is late getting to church. Sometimes Judas had a place: he was made of straw **and** was left at the church tower to be burnt on Easter Saturday.

When one was back home, one's 'palm' would keep harm away. In the Oberpfalz the head of each household would eat three buds of pussy-willow on behalf of his family, and at Rippoldsau in the Black Forest the tall cross-shaped 'palm' with its fluttering red ribbons was buried with much ceremony near the family residence; and in some places twigs from the 'palm' were planted in the fields to ward off lightning.

34

Easter Week
Karwoche

Popular custom has found nothing to do on the Monday and Tuesday, but on 'crooked Wednesday', *krumme Mittwoch* (when Judas is supposed to have hanged himself), Westphalians 'take fasting-time and (w)ring its neck off', while children in the Herford district used to hang ring-shaped pretzels on willow switches and sing:

> Palm, palm, poke,
> Let the cuckoo croak,
> Let the birdies sing
> As our palms we bring.

> *Palm, Palm, Posken*
> *Lot den Kuckuck rosken*
> *Lot die Vüegel singen*
> *Lot de Palmen springen.*

Gründonnerstag, 'green Thursday' (the colour green was a symbol of being cleansed from sin) was the day for cleaning the house, brushing one's clothes and taking a bath. And one would eat green things—chives, herbs and spinach—and honey for breakfast: people in Hamburg and the Harz hills like rolls filled with honey and call them *Judasohren*, 'Judas' ears'. Try an egg laid on Green Thursday—it will do you a world of good, and if its brother egg hatches out the bird will change the colour of its feathers every year.

Good Friday, *Karfreitag* or *stille Freitag*, has generally been a quiet fast-day in Germany, although in the Eifel hills a splendid procession with tableaux vivants of Bible scenes marched for all

35

to see—Samson slaying the Philistines with the jawbone of an ass, Jonah in the fish's belly, Jesus with the twelve apostles; but it became 'too worldly' and was banned by 1800. Good Friday is a good day for sowing flowers; if you cut your hair on Good Friday it will grow strong and thick; if you cool a hot iron in 'Good Friday water' it will cure warts; and Westphalians say that rain on Good Friday will 'bless the whole year'.

On Easter Saturday Westphalian boys would gather at midnight to 'hunt the Judas' with much stamping and ear-splitting noise from wooden rattles. In Silesia the bell-ringer came to put out the candles before the morning service and then, wearing a red waistcoat, became Judas and was driven out of the church by the village children.

The dramatic change from mourning to triumph is heralded in the Tyrol early on Easter morning, when a fire is lit with flint and steel before the church door. From this new fire the church candles are lighted afresh and the villagers bring lighted faggots back to their homes before returning to witness the events of Easter Sunday with all its colour, candles and flowers, the purple victor's robe and the white Easter flag, the crash of trumpets and organ music and the joyous ringing of bells.

Easter

Ostern

THE GERMAN EASTER is a great gesture of triumph over death and darkness. One laughed at the powers of evil, preachers even joked about it—Johann Mathesius, a friend of Luther's, described how Christ came to the door of Hell, which two devils were trying to bolt with their long noses; but Jesus knocked so firmly on the door that the foxy devils had their snouts knocked off.

Pagan custom has survived in the form of Easter bonfires and 'Easter wheels' rolled flaming from hill-crests to the valley below. Fetch the charred remains of a burnt-out Easter wheel and spread them on your fields; it will make them fertile. Don't buy the timber for your Easter bonfire, steal it from the woods, and it will bring you better luck.

Easter eggs have been laid for centuries. Generally the Easter Hare claims to have laid them, and Swabians make him a *Hasengärtle*, a 'hare's garden', out of willow twigs and moss, for the purpose, but he has competitors: the cock, in Upper Bavaria and Austria, the stork, in Franconian Thuringia, the fox, near Hanover, the cuckoo, at Bad Salzungen, the crane, and even the capercailzie.

Eggs had been forbidden during Lent, and were the pagan symbol of fertility, two good reasons for eating plenty at Eastertime. One gave eggs as presents, and the number given had a meaning in the Eifel, where one egg given by a girl to her young man meant 'what a pity' and six meant 'time to get married'. In Sweden, courting couples would blow eggs, paint them with flowers and fill them with rolled-up slips of paper inscribed with wishes, verses and terms of endearment before presenting them.

Games with Easter eggs abound: finding them, rolling them downhill, or playing 'conkers' with them as though they were chestnuts, and one played on into Easter Monday. But Easter food was serious and was taken to church to be blessed: eggs, bread, salt and meat. The most typical thing to eat at Easter is the Easter loaf, a kind of unleavened bread in various shapes—the Alemannic quartered *Schild*, the East Frisian *Plas-kes*, the Saxon *Quarkkeilchen*, the Swabian *Ostergeigen*, the Upper Bavarian *Osterlaibl*, the Pomeranian *Osterwolf* with its four paws and open mouth, and the enormous Viennese *Osterkuchen*.

Horses had an Easter airing too. Young men at Höxter in Westphalia would meet at the church on horseback and ride off in a body, then suddenly break ranks and gallop, each for himself, towards a cross-shaped winning-post. One did not have to bother about damage, since Easter rides are good for the crops,

and the prize was a valuable cake, baked in the shape of a horse—a Westphalian horse, naturally. If you lived near Traunstein you would go on the *Georgi-Ritt* and ride with St. George on his white horse to Ettendorf church on Easter Monday; and this ride is now a pageant with knights, men-at-arms, heralds and fanfares.

Even running water was infected with magic at Easter time, provided you rose before sunrise and scooped it up in a downstream direction, and you had to do it silently—if you made a noise it was *Plapperwasser*, 'babble-water', and would do you no good. And at Hildesheim belief ran strong that running water turned at an unexpected moment on Easter night into wine. There were citizens who were prepared to wait all night on their stomachs with their tongues in a local brook for the magic moment to arrive.

Driving out the Cattle
Viehaustrieb

IF YOU OWNED cattle in a German village you might well be wakened by the blast of a horn at six in the morning and warned to get your beasts ready. The parish cowherd would take them over, and as he did so would tap the calves with a sprig of mountain ash, changing the baby names like *Mütsken* or *Bütsken* into the sonorous names of cowhood—*Blesse*, perhaps, or *Stern* or *Silwernelle* or *Hiätteblume*. If it was your turn to supply the cowherd's lunch, your good wife would prepare some hard-boiled eggs and use the empty shells to decorate the ash sprig, which was hung, bright with coloured ribbons and buttercups, over the cowhouse door. She would put the eggs and the tin of bread and butter into the cowherd's *Holster*, his satchel, which he had left hanging outside the night before together with his staff of office, his *Klingerstock*, which had a metal loop on it loaded with clanking rings. In the morning he would call for both and take the cattle off.

An East Frisian cowherd was elected for a year by the parish and paid in cash, wool, milk, cheese, clothes, boots and any special clothing he needed for his job. He was proud of his position and would chat to the pastor as an equal.

The Witches' Sabbath

Walpurgisnacht

WITCHES began to be invented and hunted in Germany in the fifteenth century, when the Papal Inquisitor Jakob Sprenger was given the job of witch-detection North of the Alps. Protestant belief made no difference, and the myths of witches' characteristics multiplied in Germany as elsewhere. Witches, one knew for certain, rubbed themselves with a gruesome ointment compounded of fat, deadly nightshade, opium, hemlock and other horrors, after which they would go into a trance and wake to recount their exploits.

The Brocken, the highest mountain in Northern Germany, was the witches' favourite rendezvous. They would fly or ride there, obliging the Devil by gnawing a piece off each church-bell they passed, land on the Brocken and begin by dancing the snow away. Thunder and lightning would be laid on as they swooped to the witches' altar and the devil's pulpit for their Black Mass,

first kissing the Devil's cloven hoof. Proceedings went on till the first cock-crow.

You could tell a witch sometimes by seeing a red mouse hop out of her mouth, and if you could overhear her say the password you could get in to a Witches' Sabbath. The long hooked nose, bushy eyebrows joined in the middle, and hump back were fixed in people's minds by folk-tales.

Anti-witch precautions varied: you could bang the ground in front of your house with a plank and shout 'Witch get out, the house is burning'; you could put your goats in different stalls so that witches could not find them; you could hide your brooms, depriving witches of their transport, lay stockings crosswise on children's beds, paint treble crosses over doors, or stand a broom upside down on your threshold.

In 1701 the learned Christian Thomasius made some headway against witch-hunting with his *Dissertatio de crimine magiae*, but in 1715 the legal faculty of Tübingen sent another witch to the stake, and the last German-speaking witch was executed, at Glarus in Switzerland, as late as 1782.

May Day
Maitag

YOUNG GIRLS in Anhalt used to rise before dawn on May Day to wash their freckles in dew and utter charms to make them go away. Young men in many districts would make a *Maien* out of birch twigs, tinsel and artificial flowers, and get up early to hang it under their sweetheart's window. Westphalian farmers would even decorate their dunghills with green branches, and were pleased if it rained on May Day 'because it would kill the plantains'. 'May water' is magical and needs care and respect, so the children at Altenrath on the Agger would clean the village brook at midnight, decorate it with flowers and then walk from house to house singing *Bonne gefaech, Bonne gefaech* ('The brook is swept').

In Thuringian villages the children used to 'fetch Spring from the woods': a boy would hide in a thicket and when they had found him they would deck him with green leaves and escort him home in triumph. In Schleswig-Holstein they pay court to the *Maigräfin*, the 'May Countess', and her partner the *Maigraf;* elsewhere she is called the 'May Bride' or the 'May Queen'.

Apprentices of Bochum have had a fine procession on May

Day since 1398, when Count Engelbert III expressed his gratitude for their assistance in a local feud by granting them the right to cut a large oak-tree once a year from the Bockolt forest near Harpen and to celebrate on the proceeds. They are still celebrating, in peaked caps and blue-and-white sashes.

A maypole is a serious matter: Bavarians would pick a suitable tree-trunk in February, peel the bark off in spiral patterns, and hang as many as thirty carved figures up the stem. The girls were called in to decorate the fat tyre-shaped wreath with flowers and ribbons before it was hauled to the top. Sometimes the wreath had little presents in it, and boys would climb for them with pitch on their bare feet. You had to put a guard on your maypole in case a neighbouring parish thought of stealing it. Reports of German maypoles, dances round maypoles, and attempts to ban them, go back seven hundred years.

May Day is only one of the occasions when the joy of spring

44

erupts into the German calendar. At Antdorf, South of the Starnberger See, they have a 'spring running', the *Mailaufen*, every three years on the first Sunday in May. The girls are 'rounded up' and advance in a body to music across a meadow towards the young men, who wait sitting on a bench with their backs to the girls, accompanied by two brooms and a stable lantern. At a given signal the girls rush to the bench and tip it over; in the ensuing scuffle each grabs a boy by the hand, and since by custom there are three more boys than girls, the three boys left out have to dance with a broom or a stable lantern each.

Ascension Day   Whitsun
Christi Himmelfahrt   *Pfingsten*

ASCENSION DAY is a great occasion in the Tyrol, when the figure of Christ is drawn up into the church roof to the sound of trumpets. And it is supposed to rain, as the heavens have opened to let Jesus through. Superstition also alleges a tendency to rain on Thursdays in deference to the old god Thor, and it was inadvisable to work in the fields (and also, curiously, to take a bath) on any Thursday in the year. In Berlin and elsewhere, husbands go on a stag outing called a *Herrenpartie*.

At Whitsun the Holy Ghost comes down through the round opening in the roofs of many Tyrolese churches: a gilded wheel with the carved figure of a dove which circles lower and lower. Most Whit custom is however pagan, an open-air festival, not really separate from May Day—Silesians waited for Whitsun to put up their maypole. In many districts villagers went into the woods to collect green branches and came back with a green-clad

figure with a mask made of tree-bark: he is called *Pfingstl* in the
South, and in Thuringia the Wild Man or Green Man (*Laub-
männchen*); sometimes he wears a bird-like mask, has to be
splashed with water and is called the water-bird, the *Wasservogel*.

In the Goldene Aue district, in the Harz, they look for the May
King, who is masked and wears a golden crown hung with bells,
and must guess who he is: each time someone guesses wrong, he
rings the bells by shaking his head.

Near Erfurt they would bury the greenery which the 'leafy
king' had worn in the flax fields to make them fertile, and at
Langensalza in Thuringia they called the Green Man 'Whit-cart'
(*Pfingstkarr*) to match the custom of racing to the maypole with
one's girl in a wheelbarrow. Down in Swabia the schoolchildren
would spend Whit Monday singing their way round the village,
with blackened faces and hats made of green wheat, collecting
eggs, bacon, sausages, wine and pretzels in buckets.

The Tyrolese have no maypole and no May King, but cele-

46

brate Whit Saturday by eating 'May butter', a formidable mixture of cream, butter, sugar and cinnamon, followed by whip-cracking competitions lasting until midnight. Elsewhere young men dress up, mount horses and compete at *Kranzstechen*, tilting at a wreath hung from a decorated arch. The winner is the 'Whit King' (*Pfingstkönig*) and the worst performer the 'Whit-Boy' (*Pfingstjunge*). Thuringian girls would play at 'Banging the Pot' (*Topfschlagen*), a sort of blind man's buff, trying to find a pot blindfolded and bang it with a wooden spoon. Cowherds would play various games involving being first or last out to the pasture: the first beast out, or sometimes the last, became the 'Whit-Ox' (*Pfingstochse*) and was wreathed with flowers, and in Westphalia the cowherds would try to nail up their rivals' stable-doors so that someone else would be the last to get his cattle out and thus earn the title of *Pennbuck* ('Sleepy Billy') and the privilege of being ridden through the village on a log wearing a huge crown of green branches, yellow broom and tulips.

The Marksmen's Fair
Schützenfest

GERMAN MARKSMEN have been organised since the days when the Emperor Henry I founded Imperial cities and encouraged the inhabitants to practise the longbow in case of local war. Much the same occurred in England, and the yew-trees planted to provide timber for the bows still grow in our churchyards. Very early on the German amateur marksmen succeeded in acquiring guild status, and have preserved their guild houses and privileges through the days of the longbow, the crossbow and the musket

47

to the present time. Their usefulness as a military force was taken
from them by the creation of a standing army in the seventeenth
century, but they carried on undeterred with target-shooting, or
shooting at a 'bird' on top of a tall pole, and particularly with all
the accompanying festivities.

Marksmen's guilds were hierarchic and full of rules; presided
over by a Captain or a Master, they also had a Treasurer to look
after their valuables, and particularly a *Pritschenmeister* to organise
the shooting, get the crowd laughing and bang inferior marksmen
with his harlequin's sword.

Regrettable lapses from decorum have been chronicled. In
1458 Lucerne were shooting against Constance, one of whose men

let slip the word 'cow', whereupon the outraged Lucerners seized the village of Weinfelden; and in 1509 the Cologne team attempted to cheat the winner Hans Sindelfinger, a Stuttgart tailor, of the hundred guilders he had fairly won, and the great Götz von Berlichingen, the iron-handed champion of liberty, had to intervene to make them disgorge.

Nevertheless, great efforts were made to encourage respectability. One guild imposed a sixpenny fine for all 'oaths, blasphemy and the naming of the Devil', and in Friesland delinquents were fined in beer, although a fine of half a jug was not likely to improve the condition of 'those unable to get home on their own legs'.

Whit Monday was preferred for a Fair, in spite of a complaint by the Church dated 1578 that it interfered with church business. The Marksmen would march to their 'Marksman King's' house in their colourful uniforms and fetch him with much pomp, first to the Guild House and then to the butts, where results would

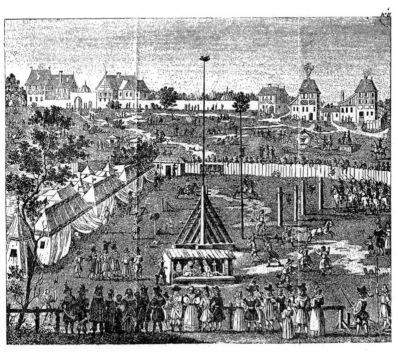

49

decide a new King. A proper Fair lasts not less than three days and not longer than three weeks, and nearly every town in West-phalia has one. Bavarian Marksmen wear particularly splendid decorated hats. Near Paderborn, so Annette Droste-Hülshoff records, they used to reserve the second day for the ladies, and the winner became *Scheibenkönigin*, 'Target Queen', chose a King-Consort and held court.

The Fairs developed into great open-air shows with dozens of side-shows and fun for young and old, and one of the proudest was the Dresden 'Bird Meadow', the *Vogelwiese*, parallel to but much older than the October Fair at Munich. Founded in 1446, the Dresden Archers' Society organised their fair for centuries from the year 1459. First the tall 'bird-poles' were set up with much ceremony; a lavish banquet followed, then the cross-bow marksmanship, and after prizes had been awarded the competitors went round the side-shows and stayed till after dark to watch the fireworks.

Weddings
Hochzeit

A FULL-BLOWN GERMAN COUNTRY WEDDING demands accuracy in elaborate detail, the endurance of a mountaineer and the digestion of a goat. Begin with a good *Polterabend*, the party the night before, to drive away evil spirits: get the crowd to split the air with noise—smash old crockery, bang pots together, crack whips until you're dizzy.

You may send written invitations rich in art work, but the country custom of sending out the *Hochzeitslader*, the 'wedding-

inviter', or *Köstenbidder* as they call him in Lower Saxony, is more personal. Get him into his Sunday best, decorate him with flowers and ribbon, give him his stick with a wreath on it to knock at the doors, and off he goes. He will be well, too well, received, and may never reach the last house, but the word will have spread.

Another way is to go round with your bride-to-be and invite the guests yourself. Take little presents, especially for the god-parents, in exchange for the useful things they are giving for your household. In Baden the bride used to receive a 'lucky loaf', a *Glücksbrot,* and would crumble some of it into the first pot of soup she made as a housewife. In Swabia the bride-to-be would go round with a basket of handkerchiefs and gave one to each invited guest.

Then, if you are the bride, the furniture has to be driven to your future home. The horses or oxen, the driver and even the wagon must be dressed as for the wedding itself. If you like, send a few musicians in front. Pile your wagon high with furniture and a gaily painted 'bridal chest' containing your trousseau and the rest of your dowry, and do not forget your spinning-wheel and a distaff with flax on it (in Silesia, the higher your distaff

Der Blünder-Wagen zur Egerländer Bauern Hochzeit.

stuck out from the other goods, the richer you were supposed to be). Make a good show of an immense double bed and a cradle as well, and get your waggon to the door at twelve o'clock sharp. The groom will be on the threshold to meet you, jug of beer in hand: give him a pair of shoes, a shirt that you have spun and woven yourself, and the key to your bridal chest.

Two days later at most, you should be getting married, but mind the day of the week. Don't choose a day in Lent or Advent, or a Wednesday; if you come from South Germany, avoid a Friday, but in the North, prefer it. Tuesday and Thursday are two good days, but mind that the moon is waxing and not on the wane, and that you get to church before noon so that the sunlight is waxing too. A nasty day bodes misfortune, except in some districts, where if the bride's dress is rained on 'she will be showered with luck and bonny children'.

The bride will have to fit herself into a wedding-dress handed down from generation to generation and endure the construction of an elaborate wedding crown. It is made of wire, tinsel, artificial flowers, pearls, ribbon, and pins: in 1911 one bride from the Spree Forest sat in a chair from one in the morning onwards while her milliner dressed her hair and made her headdress, using 2,783 pins. Don't try on another girl's bridal wreath, or you will stay a spinster, and don't take your own wreath off before midnight, or misfortune will stalk your marriage.

The wedding day starts off with a breakfast called 'morning soup' or 'bridal soup', which includes other liquids, in the bride's and bridegroom's homes. Many guests attend these meals, after which the groom is escorted to fetch his bride, and he needn't expect to do that easily. Sometimes the bride is hidden, and he has to find her, or in Bavaria he is greeted first by a bearded man in bridal dress (designed to deceive not only the unfortunate groom but evil spirits as well). Near Bückeburg the bridesmaids would dress exactly the same as the bride for the same purpose.

Once the groom has his bride by the hand, he puts her in the wedding cart and drives to the church, but he should have some money with him to pay toll to young men who may seize his horse on the way.

53

As bride and groom walk up the aisle they should keep close together to leave no room for evil spirits to slip in between, and they should keep their eyes on the ground and not look about them, or they may make eyes at other people when they are man and wife. As both kneel to be blessed, the bridegroom can indicate his intention of keeping his bride in order by kneeling on the hem of her dress. The bride can assert herself by treading on the groom's foot as she gets up (this was reported by one Werner, an Augustine monk, in 1250) and either can try as they clasp hands to keep his or her own hand uppermost.

Then home, on foot in the South and in North Germany generally in a horse and cart. The horse will trot all the merrier, it is said, if you give him a little brandy. Remember to guard the groom against heavy drinking—throw a beer-jug over the roof; and shut the gate and the front door, and make the hungry guests hand over little presents to get in. Avoid the evil spirits waiting under the threshold by carrying your bride across, and once you have her inside, share a bite of bread with her, as they did in Pomerania, and you will never go short of food. Your mother should throw rice or dried peas over the bride: the number of grains which stick in her dress will show how many children you can expect. Push your bride into the kitchen: the first thing she must do now that she is a housewife is to put salt in the soup.

And now, the wedding breakfast proper. Be prudent and arrange transport to fetch the ingredients in advance. A Pomeranian wedding in 1907 consumed 32 hundredweight of flour, 4 swine, 2 calves, 3 sheep, 32 geese, 8 hundredweight of large fish, 10 hundredweight of small fish, 54 barrels of beer, 500 bottles of wine and 300 litres of brandy. Nothing was left, since guests at a big farmhouse wedding would run into hundreds.

In case your guests really cannot eat all that is put before them, provide a napkin for them to take titbits home in. The Bavarians

call this a *B'schoadtüchl*; it is of decent size, in blue and red checks. In Schaumburg-Lippe the head of the house sits with the *Frit-Esser*, the 'free eaters', honoured guests such as the pastor, the schoolmaster and the magistrate, who do not have to pay little presents to come in. It is a great honour, which you cannot refuse, to be a Free Eater.

The 'wedding inviter' next begins to function as a toastmaster. He drinks the health of the bride and groom, throws his glass over his shoulder and takes care that it smashes noisily to bring good luck, and goes on to insist on the rapid production of half-a-dozen bouncing sons. Then he introduces the guests by name, and as they step forward and offer their presents, the bridegroom offers each of them a drink from a jug. The music strikes up for dancing, but before the bride takes the floor, she complains that her shoe hurts, pulls it off and finds a coin in it, which she gives to the band. Then she leads off with the groom, followed by the parents. The dancing shakes down the first courses and gives the assembly courage to finish the enormous meal, but before they do, the cook appears with a 'burnt' hand in a bandage, asks for 'some money for medicine' and is handed her tip.

In Hessen one of the guests watches his chance to pin the end of a long roll of red ribbon to the bride's stocking. When it

unrolls across the floor everybody cheers, and she has to cut it up into scraps, one for each guest to wear like a medal.

At midnight the bride is blindfolded, her wreath taken off and her hair, the symbol of her unmarried state, covered with a bonnet. The bridegroom, the best man (called the *Brautführer*) and the bridesmaids dance round the bride in a circle. Still blindfolded, she must catch one of the bridesmaids: the one she catches will be the first to marry. The bonnet must be placed on the bride's head by married women, and she must at first pretend to resist. Then she must dance with all the bridegroom's male relatives in turn round three candles placed on the floor. If the candles are not blown out by the dancing, the marriage will be a smooth one.

North German weddings used to end with a 'sweep-out', a *Kehraus*, danced by the guests to polanaise time as they beat time with household utensils and followed each other, always to the same tune, round the house and out through the outbuildings. The guests see the happy couple home to their new house and even into their new bedroom. Franconians would forestall evil spirits, the 'bad people', by putting three pieces of bread and three lumps of coal into a corner of the marriage-bed. Elsewhere they put pieces of bread under the bed so that the children born of the marriage would have good teeth.

Bride and groom might try to slip away from the wedding,

but the band would be on the look-out and run after them, *Heimblasen,* 'blowing them home'.

At last, sometime that night, they would be alone. Would-be rejoicers at other people's weddings would have to wait seven years at least to celebrate again, and perhaps not then, as some districts mistrust the 'bad seven', the *böse Sieben;* but the Rose Wedding will be due in ten years, Silver in twenty-five, Gold in fifty and Diamond in sixty.

Babies

'A WOMAN with child should be served by angels' preached a Silesian monk in the fourteenth century, and mothers-to-be, midwives and even fathers-to-be have been privileged throughout German history. The father would be released from work even to fetch his wife frivolous things to eat and drink.

Stories to satisfy the impatient small brother or sister have described the stork carrying the baby from as far off as Egypt; or (in the Harz) a turkey 'scratching the baby out of the gatepost'; or the midwife (in Switzerland) 'fetching' the baby from the 'milky spring', the *Milchbrünnli;* or the baby 'coming away' from the spring near St. Kunibert's Church at Cologne 'where Mary plays all day with the babies and gives them nice pudding to eat'.

Mummy has plenty to think of while she is waiting. Don't look at ugly things; don't stand about in front of the bread-cupboard, or your child will go hungry; don't drink spirits, or it will 'burn his heart out'; don't rock the empty cradle 'or you'll take his sleep away'. Endure your toothache, it will do him good.

Women near their time in Saxony used to like helping a mare in labour, reckoning that they might be rewarded with an easy delivery themselves. Germans traditionally keep an eye on the signs of the Zodiac prevailing at their birth: Goethe carefully noted his in *Dichtung und Wahrheit*. 'Wise women' neglected stars in favour of signs gathered from the sun, moon, wind or clouds. Mind the date you're born on: the first of April was Judas' birthday (and Bismarck's too, for that matter). It is lucky to be born after midnight, but also lucky to be born at any hour and to have a tree planted for you. Goethe's grandfather planted a birch-tree for him in his garden at Frankfurt.

Camomile tea was reckoned to be good for a woman in labour, or coffee, or raisins in brandy if you lived in Friesland. When the new-born infant had produced his first cry, a Munich mid-wife would wrap him in his father's shirt to make the child love his father. In Württemberg and Alsace they would lay the baby on the ground for his father to pick him up in recognition. In Hessen they would put him on a horse, to make him able to survive any fever. Westphalian grandmothers would put a piece of baked apple into the baby's mouth 'to give him the right to live, once he'd eaten human food' and incidentally to give him sweet breath for life.

Mothers in the Eifel would sing this variant of an ancient lullaby:

> Sleep, baby, sleep,
> Father's got the sheep,
> Mother's got the coloured cow,
> Baby shut your eyes now,
> Sleep, baby, sleep.

> *Schlof, Kendche, schlof,*
> *dei Vader hit de Schof,*
> *dei Muder hit de blimelich Kuh,*
> *Kendchen dun deng Äujelcher zu,*
> *Schlof, Kendche, schlof.*

Baby was swaddled, firmly wrapped like a mummy with crossed arms. Drop a gold coin into his first bath and he'll be rich, then pour the bathwater on the ground under a rose-bush or a young fruit-tree, and he'll grow as the tree does. Wait for the first Thursday when the moon is on the wax, and before you bath him rub him all over with fat, dust him with flour, rub it off with a dry cloth and he'll always have a good skin and never get pimples (this was a Bavarian tip). Keep a light burning in his room at all times, as the evil *Wichtelmänner* who seize children from their cradles and leave changelings in their place can only see in the dark. Paint a cloven hoof on his cradle in case a witch tries her luck on him before he is christened.

Meanwhile Mother would stay at home; until she was churched she should not leave the shelter of her home roof. Her relatives and women friends would come with a *Weisat,* a little parcel of sugar, coffee, butter and eggs. She went for her churching, the *Vorsegnung,* about six weeks after her child was born. Then she could take him out, and the neighbouring housewives would give him a *Schwatzei,* a 'chatter-egg', and tap him on the mouth with it to make it easier for him to learn to talk.

Christenings
Taufe

SOME GERMAN CHRISTENINGS take place at home and some in church. The godfather is important because the child may take after him, as they think in the Rhineland, or 'a ninth part of him' as used to be said in Hildburghausen. Godfathers have been known as a *Göd, Got, Pate* or *Gevatter,* and you have to pair your godfather with a godmother to symbolise a happy marriage when the child grows up. Near Minden you invited five godparents, and in the Sauerland 'god-aunts' and 'god-uncles' by the dozen, who all brought christening presents accompanied by gaily painted 'christening letters'.

'Godfathering is glory for the Lord and hard on your pocket' they used to say, and you couldn't refuse the honour, but in Thuringia you could put your *Gevatterbrief,* your invitation to the christening, in your window and thus hint to parents-to-be that this year at least your services had been booked.

Don't let strangers know the baby's name before he is christened, give him a nickname instead—in the Palatinate they called all boys 'pan-handle', *Pfannenstielche*, and all girls *Bohnenblättche*, 'bean-leaf'. Pinch your godchild lightly in the arm at the christening, it will bring him luck. Don't christen boys and girls in the same water. Brothers and sisters will always love each other if they are christened by the light of the same candle, so pick a large and heavy candle as they used to do at Berchtesgaden and there will still be a stump left for the last of the family. If the youngest godfather carries the child home at a brisk pace he will have no trouble learning to walk.

At the christening lunch in Silesia the pastor said grace at the head of a long table. The men sat on one side and the women on the other, the schoolmaster ladled out the soup, and the father filled the glasses; there were jokes about 'drinking him dry', and a beer-barrel stood outside the house to announce free beer to passers-by.

Sometimes pairs of German christian names contribute syllables towards a nickname: Elise and Charlotte make Lilo.

Le Batême des Lutheriens à Augsbourg. Die Tauf Ceremonie, der Lutheraner in Augspurg

Topping Out
Richtfest

WHEN THE LAST ROOF-TIMBER of your new house goes on in Germany, big house or small, town or country, you must give a party for the men. In the North you hang up a wreath called a *Richtkrone*, in the South a decorated bush like a Christmas tree.

Bavarian carpenters used to haul the heavy roof-timbers up by hand to the rhythm of the untranslatable Carpenter's Litany:

> *Ja—an ianda hörts,*
> *Ja—so fürwärts,*
> *Ja—dös feichta Holz,*
> *Ja—da auffi soll's,*
> *Ja—da auffi muass,*
> *Ja—is unsa Buass:* and much more.

You may find that your topmost roof-beam has vanished in the night. Send out a search-party and you will find it in a neighbouring village, beautifully decorated. You will have to bargain lengthily before it can be brought back in style, drawn by six oxen encouraged by a concertina-player and preceded by a man in a top hat riding on a horse.

Once the beam is back in place you can celebrate. One of the carpenters stands on the roof and becomes the *Polier*, the 'speaker'; he relates in verse his thanks to God, 'the highest builder in Heaven'; asks for blessings on the house and all those who will live in it; thanks the masons and carpenters; and finally drinks three healths to the house-owner and his family, throwing the glass to the ground, where it must smash properly to prevent bad luck. In the Spree forest they wrote down the 'speaker's' verse blessing and nailed it to the roof-beam.

63

After the ceremony all the men went to the nearest inn and ate and drank with the owner and his family and friends. In olden times every neighbour used to contribute something to a new house: horses' heads to put on the gables, carved beams inscribed with coloured mottos, or handsome windows painted with portraits of the donor and his wife, or the house-owner and his lady. In North Germany you broke off work when the windows had gone in and invited your friends round for a 'window-pane beer'.

Corpus Christi

Fronleichnam

THIS IS THE OCCASION for splendid religious processions in the open air, ecclesiastical pomp and colour, the joyful ringing of church bells, music, and in some places, carpets of flowers for the procession to walk over. Altars decked with flowers and candles are set up and services held in the open. Guilds carry their banners and the Marksmen's Guilds fire salutes. At Mühlheim near Cologne the procession takes to the Rhine in steamers and barges bright with flags, and on the Chiemsee a fleet of boats row gently while the home-made cannon, called *Böller*, bang away, the people sing and the bands play.

This is also the day when the little town of Furth puts on its *Drachenstich*, the fight with the dragon. The monster has been on

5—ACOGC

the town's strength for nearly four hundred years; the citizens have hotly defended the right to keep him, in spite of official disapproval, and the authorities have been persuaded to subsidise the animal—red cloth for his tongue, wages for the men inside and yellow dye for their stockings. That was in the seventeenth century, and they managed to keep him fighting every year on Corpus Christi Day until 1886, when they were obliged to move him to the second Sunday in August to avoid a total ban. Slyly the dragon's protagonists pointed out that the crowds watching this thirst-provoking contest would be drinking white beer from the Elector's own brewery, and the pageant was re-written to give it patriotic overtones. So the dragon survives, although he is no longer led to battle on a chain by mounted knights, followed by a lady in a palanquin.

About 1912 the dragon was not much to look at—'rather like a cow with wings', but some resourceful citizens bought one of Wagner's dragons second-hand in Munich for 30 marks, and he served Furth valiantly until 1939. Furth has now built a new dragon worthy of the space age: over 50 feet long, 9 feet high and weighing over 18 hundredweight. He breathes fire, flaps his wings, belches smoke and rushes headlong at his adversary, propelled by his own private motor.

The Fishermen's Jousting-Match at Ulm

Ulmer Fischerstechen

AT SOME TIME in history, it is not clear when, fisher-boys of the Free Imperial City of Ulm began to hold jousting-matches on the Danube. They may have been granted the privilege by King Albert II of Habsburg in 1438, were in any case told by the municipality to stop it in 1545, and were at it again for the amusement of Philip of Spain in 1549. At first the games were held on Ash Wednesday, then at Easter, and finally at the end of July for Kermesse. A fortnight beforehand they would visit the burgomaster, solemnly ask his permission to hold their games, and hand him a basket of fish in exchange for his gracious consent.

Das Ulmer Fischerstechen am 10 August 1818.

On the great day they would dress up in extravagant costumes and walk through the town, their sweethearts by their sides all dressed in white. They carried the *Hauptspeer*, a lance from which dangled silver prizes for the winners—watches, goblets, candlesticks and spoons—presented by local burghers.

Spectators were accommodated on the bank or on strings of boats moored in the stream. Trumpets played and drums beat out the 'Water March' as the jousting-boats pulled out from either bank and faced each other in midstream. The boatmen were dressed all in white, while the contestants standing on the twelve inches of thwart at the stern of each boat were dressed to contrast with their opponents—farmer against farmer's wife, two fools against one another, alderman and cowhand, Faust and Mephistopheles. Each contestant, balancing his long, blunt-ended wooden lance, attempted to strike his opponent on the left side of the chest. As one after the other of the gaily-dressed jousters plunged into the river or fell into his own boat, the band played the Ulm Fishermen's March, allegedly composed by the Emperor Charles V on a visit to the city. The last man on his feet was the 'King' of the Games; he appeared in his jousting costume at a great ball and had the right to dance with all the beauties of Ulm.

The Passion Plays

Passionsspiele

ONE VERY MODEST TRADITION of presenting a Passion Play has been running every ten years at Erl in the Tyrol since the seventeenth century. It was at one time so economical that the performers' costumes only covered their workaday clothes at the front, so that they could never turn their backs on the audience.

In contrast, Oberammergau's Passion Play has grown to lavish size. It began when the village was threatened by the Black Death in the seventeenth century and the inhabitants swore an oath that

Perspectivische Ansicht der Schaubühne zu Oberammergau bej der Vorstellung des Passions. 1840

if they were spared, they would perform a Passion Play every ten years for ever. With a few interruptions they have done so ever since, performing in the church, then on open ground, and since 1900, by which time the Play had been world-famous for decades, in their own open-air theatre.

Today the players, who are all amateurs and inhabitants of the village, use a nineteenth-century text and music written by the village schoolmaster in the year of Waterloo. The women, who must be unmarried, all wear their hair long, and the men begin to grow their hair and beards a year in advance—all except the actor who plays Pilate. Judas is perhaps the best actor's part, and there is a tradition that the man who plays Christ takes the Prologue part in ten years' time. The costumes are lavish, but there is no make-up and no artificial lighting. The audience sit under cover, which accentuates the natural light on the huge classical stage. If it rains the actors play on, with waterproof shirts under their costumes.

The play begins before nine in the morning and goes on, with a mid-day break, for nearly eight hours, in many acts, each divided into three parts: first a spoken and sung prologue by the great choir; then a tableau, shown inside the central building, of a scene in the Old Testament; and finally a realistically acted scene of the episode in the New Testament foretold in the tableau. The scenes run from Christ driving out the money-changers in the Temple, up to the Resurrection.

The Passion Play is due next in 1970, running from May to September, twice a week. Visitors to the Play stay two nights, often in the long-haired and bearded performer's houses. The inhabitants are by tradition soft-spoken and gentle-mannered.

St. John's Day

Johannistag

MIDSUMMER DAY was lucky or the reverse, according to your district, but there was plenty to do besides worry. In Northern Thuringia they would hang wreaths on their doors, because that night John the Baptist would walk through the streets and bow to any door with a wreath on it. Vaguely connected with St. John and the Jordan was the Saxon custom (at Reichenbach) of throwing a maypole into the water together with one of the dancers, who once fished out was firmly named Johannes.

Not only water, but fire: bonfires on the hilltops; flaming wheels rolled from hillcrests into the valleys; empty tar-barrels set alight and swung on a rope in wild circles. If you lived in the Harz and jumped over one of these, you would enjoy good health and a good harvest. Are you looking for a sign that you will be lucky in love? Grasp your sweetheart by the hand and leap over a fire, don't let go and don't let your clothes catch alight, and all will be well. If you are a girl, live in the Harz and want to say 'yes', hang a corn-flower wreath outside your house, and if you mean 'no', put thistles in it.

The Midsummer Fires would make the crops grow, and if you drove cattle across the ashes they would be safe from disease or accident. While Midsummer Fires were burning you had to do without fire in your kitchen, and even the village smith had to let his forge grow cold.

In the Harz they decorated larch-trees with coloured eggs, flowers and all kinds of pretty things; small 'St. John's Trees' were carried through the streets by children in the afternoon, and in the evening they were lit up, there was much dancing, and young men could kiss their sweethearts under them. Gaiety, sausage-stands and beer: the 'Harz Carnival'.

Elderberry blossoms, *Hulasträubla*, are the property of St. John, and in the Egerland people would fry them and eat them.

The Shepherd's Race at Markgröningen

Schäferlauf

NEARLY EVERY OTHER GERMAN CRAFT or profession holds its *Tag* or congress. The numbers of German shepherds have dwindled and their *Tag* is no more, but the Shepherd's Race down in Baden-Württemberg on the 24th of August goes back to the fourteenth century and may be the oldest craftsmen's race in Europe. It is a fine spectacle as well, beginning with the old Shepherd's March played on trumpets and fifes as the crowd

make their way to the Church of St. Bartholomew. The shepherd lads and girls have to race 300 yards barefoot, and over stubble at that; what is more, the girls race with a pot of water on their heads and must not spill any. The winners wear crowns of plaited straw set with 'jewels' of coloured ribbon, and march proudly, with two garlanded and ribboned sheep by their side, at the head of the procession back to the town. Never mind the sore feet: they spend the evening at the Shepherd's Dance, as an ordinance of 1651 prescribes.

Couching
Gautschen

MIDSUMMER DAY being dedicated to Gutenberg the great printer, all printing apprentices get the day off and go through the ordeal of being 'couched' as though they were paper going through the process of being made. Out of the bin, on to the 'couching-board': press. Two packers lay hold of the apprentice, and either dump him on a correcting-block covered with wet sponges, or merely dip his backside in a bucket of water and then swing him to shake the drops off. Once 'couched' you would receive your 'couching letter' to prove you had been through it. Many printing-shops would not take an apprentice, whatever his working record, unless he could produce his 'couching-letter'; or else they would do the 'couching' themselves.

The apprentice paid for his 'couching' in drinks all round, and was then acknowledged as a full member of his honourable profession.

74

Lady's Thirty

Frauendreissiger

THE THIRTY DAYS after August 15th, Mary's Ascension Day, are called Lady's Thirty. Swabians say that Nature is then in her kindest and most generous mood, so it is now that medicinal herbs are gathered and blessed.

People used to go out for days before to gather herbs in meadows, woods and the borders of cornfields, collecting herbs for the proper bunch, the *Marienwisch* as they called it in Cologne,

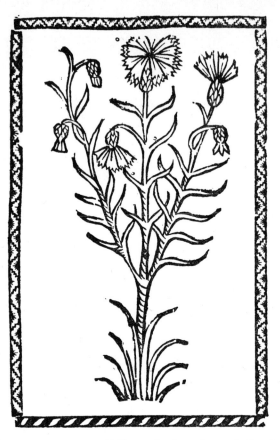

containing seventy-seven different herbs—Aaron's Rod, milfoil, vermouth, arnica and dozens more. In the Tyrol they let you off more lightly, but you had to put at least nine different herbs in each bunch, and they were carried to church in large baskets trimmed with roses and ribbons. People preferred to take their herbs to Capucin or Franciscan monks for the blessing, and would travel long distances to a monastery for the purpose. The herbs were dried and put away carefully to be used in the winter, particularly on Christmas Eve.

Years ago all the *Kräutermänner*, the herbalists, used to travel to a snow-capped peak in the Riesengebirge to have their herbs blessed at an open-air service.

Sometimes the herbs were not blessed until mid-September at the end of Lady's Thirty, leaving more time to find the rarest. Herbs provided cures for anything you might suffer from.

Hop-Picker's Supper
Hopfenmahl

BAVARIAN HOP-PICKERS are townsfolk who move, as Cockneys go to Kent, into the country for a few weeks' fresh air and some extra money. The hop-growers give them a good meal as they come in with their picking-bags, their *Rupfasackl.*

When the *Stangler* has pulled down the last string of hops and

the picking is done, the pickers decorate themselves with hop-garlands and crowd to the hop-grower's kitchen for a feast of bread soup, roast pork, potato salad and beer. The most accomplished speaker among them thanks the growers for food and lodging; then the accordion (known as as a 'mason's piano') and a mouth-organ strike up for the Hop-Picker's Dance until the 'sweep-out' at midnight.

Lambert's Day

Lambertustag (at Münster) or *Lambertitag*

ST. LAMBERT was murdered in the seventh century, and was remembered in the Middle Ages with a popular dance at Münster, where he founded the church. Young and old would dance round a pyramid of coloured lights, and the whole town would be lit up. Münster children still dance round a pyramid of lanterns made of hollowed-out beetroots covered with coloured paper and sing songs called *Lambertuslieder*.

Lambert's Day, September 17th, is also the last day for harvesting. The last sheaf of oats cut belongs to the Saint, and the reapers take it apart and bind it round the girl who gathered it. Then they lead her to the farmyard and dance, gradually plucking the oat straw off her to the strains of the lengthy ballad about 'Lazy Joe' (*Fauler Jochen*) who went to cut oats and didn't come back. Joe didn't come back, so the dog went to look for him; stick went after dog; fire went after stick; water went after fire; ox went after water; master went and had to fetch them all home. It takes some time to untangle the young lady, but she is called the *Haferbraut*, the 'oat-bride', for her pains.

79

Michaelmas
Michaelitag

St. MICHAEL is the patron Saint of Germany and by occupying the 29th of September, the day when the ancient Germans held their general assembly or *Thing* for conduct of important business, has done much to ease the old German gods out of the picture. He has always been popular, and his name may have been borrowed by that bewildered character in a white shirt and red night-cap, the 'German Michel', the caricaturists' image of the German little man.

The ancient *Thing* was an occasion for Germans to settle their affairs, and they still do important business on St. Michael's Day—servants are engaged from this date, school reports written, interest paid. In the old days craftsmen used to begin to work by artificial light, and a master gave a *Lichtgans*, a 'lighting-up goose' or a *Lichtbraten*, a 'lighting-up joint', to his apprentices.

Harvest Games
Erntefest

THERE ARE MANY THINGS to look out for and enjoy at the end of harvest—*Sichelhenke* as they call it in the South, 'time to hang your sickle up'. Give your hired hands new clothes. Leave some corn standing in the field for the 'white horse'; look out for the *Roggenmuhme*, the harvest bogy who lurks in the corn to catch children. Put the last sheaf on one side: bake bread with it and it will make your family strong; or divide it in two, put one half (marked with red ribbon) into your barn, decorate the other with ribbons, flowers and little cakes, and burn it in the open. In Bavaria this is the custom, and the young men do high-jumps over the flames.

The last wagon must have a harvest crown over it, and one of the girls must hand the crown to the owner of the farm when the wagon is back in the yard. Then you put up a carved wooden cockerel on the barn-door. In Baden, you send your musicians up to the loft, and stand a glass of water on the edge of the planks above the dancing harvesters. If a girl wants to compete for a live cockerel, she must watch her chance while dancing and lift her partner up at the right moment for him to knock the glass over. Do this three times and the cockerel is yours. The Baden girls are wonderful women.

At Crailsheim down in Württemberg they dance for a sheep, but this is luck, not skill. The couples dance round a candle in which a gold coin is embedded, and as they dance they pass a sabre from couple to couple. The couple holding the sabre at the moment when the candle burns down so low that the gold coin falls out wins the sheep, and the girl wins a silk scarf as well. The sheep is then eaten at the local inn, and the harvest crown is

discovered to be loaded with sweets and little cakes; it is stripped
of everything eatable, and the crown goes back to the farmhouse
till next year.

The Cannstatt Fair

Cannstatter Volksfest

ON 28TH SEPTEMBER 1818 William I of Württemberg remembered the famine of '16 and '17, offered prizes for the best cattle in his kingdom, organised a cattle-market, and drew attention to the fishing industry by arranging jousting-matches on the Neckar, like those at Ulm, to coincide with the Fishermen's Guild Assembly dates. Local pride in home-grown food was publicised by horse-racing on the *Wasen* meadows by the river, an extensive and attractive fairground, and a huge *Fruchtsäule*, the 'pillar of fruit', covered with local produce: in 1867 fourteen women took three weeks to dress this potent gesture against the bogy of famine.

The Fair is no longer so agricultural but remains one of the jolliest in Swabia.

Keferloh Market

Der Keferloher Markt

THE EMPEROR OTTO was so grateful to the Bavarian mounted irregulars for winning the battle of Lechfelde for him against the Hungarians in the year 955 that he knighted their captains and gave his blessing to the annual Keferloh Market on the first Sunday or Monday in September. It is a horse-fair just outside Munich and has become famous for its rowdiness. Watching jugglers, acrobats and conjurors was not enough: one trailed one's coat for a fight. Stalls even sold cudgels for the purpose, but you didn't need a stick, as the rough mugs were given away with the beer. If Bavarians want to describe a proper punch-up they still say 'just like Keferloh'.

The October Fair at Munich
Das Münchner Oktoberfest

ALLEGEDLY the largest fair in Europe, the October Fair is generally held in September to get the fine weather. Collectively it is called the *Wies'n*, the 'meadow', and covers hundreds of acres with avenues of tented stalls. The Burgomaster of Munich leads a throng of beer-wagons drawn by splendid greys, decorated carriages driven by brewers, and huge floats peopled by strong-armed waitresses, towards the first barrel, which is his by right. At noon he downs his mug and the thousands of revellers pour in: oxen are roasted whole, chickens turn on the spit and lake fish are grilled over wood-fires, while the beer flows in a mighty river.

It all goes back to 1810, when Max Joseph of Bavaria gave a generous party to celebrate the marriage of his son Ludwig to Therese of Sachsen-Hildburghausen. The celebrations were so successful that Munich City Council petitioned the King to name the *Wies'n* '*Theresia's Meadow*', and so it has been called ever since.

As at Cannstatt, the Fair included an agricultural show and horse-racing. An eye-witness, having recorded his admiration of the splendid cavalry detachments, the parades of boys and girls in peasant dress, the royal party in their pavilion (captured in battle from the Turks) and the singing of patriotic ballads, went on to describe the racing. It began with a parade of the thirty riders led by a detachment of cavalry, taking three-quarters of an hour to pass round the course, 'which was 11,200 foot long'. The winner's time in the ensuing race was 18 minutes 14 seconds, and the horse is not named, but he was a dapple-grey owned by one Franz Baumgartner.

═══════════════════════════════════════

Dürkheim Sausage Fair

Der Dürkheimer Wurstmarkt

DÜRKHEIM SAUSAGES have been publicised by the Fair for a century, and people travel there from all over the Palatinate in September. The sausages compete with the wine in this concentration of vineyards. Go into the 'greatest cask in the world' standing in the fairground; your mental arithmetic may not be able to check its claimed capacity of a million and three-quarter litres, but it is a comfortable inn, and you can be sure that the wine will not have been doctored—local rules are strict.

The fairground is lavish, musical, noisy and easy to get lost in. Since 1879 the *'Sausage Fair Advertiser'* has appeared with cartoons and poems, and a useful map to help the stragglers find their relatives.

The Grape Harvest
Weinlese

THE ROMANS may have brought vineyards to Germany, but the Germans claim to have invented the wooden cask. Wood-carvings have enriched them with coats of arms, mermaids and devils as well as vine-leaf designs, and Speyer Wine Museum has a fine collection.

As grape-picking time approaches, guard your vineyards against thieves and evil spirits, as the Tyrolese *Saltner* do at night. Few men, or devils either, could fail to be impressed by the *Saltner's* turnout. He wears a red or green tunic, a black collarless leather jacket, and a broad belt, embroidered and studded with patterns in brass rivets, slung round his hips on top of his leather breeches. You can pick him out in the dark by the white cable-stitch stockings above his leather gaiters, or by his necklace of pig's teeth and amulets known and feared by witches, but his main glory is his hat, a vast three-cornered felt construction bristling with the feathers of cocks, hens and peacocks and all a-dangle with foxes' brushes and squirrels' tails. He hardly needs his halbard or his *Rungel*, a hunting-knife with a sixteen-inch blade incised with magic signs, to persuade the 'bad people' to keep their distance.

So the grapes are picked and pressed, and although a grape-mill has replaced human feet, the spirit of the 'golden sunshine' pervades the landscape, fountains run with wine and Wine Festivals spring to life along the Rhine, the Aar and the Mosel. Drink your German wines in the open or in deep, cool, ancient cellars. If you can master the intricate names, the subtle vocabulary of appreciation, and the vigorous hospitality of the local patriots who uncork it, you will have proved a strong head and an excellent memory.

Kermesse

Kirchweih

A KERMESSE theoretically commemorates the consecration of the parish church, but has tended to become a kind of late harvest festival, often near the third Sunday in October. A tireless interest in making merry has stretched it into several days, and any spare energy can be devoted to a burst of house-cleaning and to visiting relatives.

You are supposed to celebrate Kermesse by eating at least one roast goose and two other big meals. People would send out 'inviters' as for a farm wedding, a young man called (in Swabia) a 'place-boy', a *Blotzknecht*, assisted by girls named *Blotzjungfer*.

Along the Rhine they used to dig up a bottle of wine and give it a musical escort to the inn. A young man danced in front of the band beating time with a garlanded staff, and both bottle and staff would be hung from the ceiling above the dancing, gaily drinking crowd.

Dissipate your surplus energy in the Pieter Bruegel style in the

open with anything from wrestlers to roundabouts. Along the Middle Rhine they would finish Kermesse by burying a carving of Zacchaus, the appropriate patron saint, and dig it up again to open a new Kermesse the following year.

Local Costume
Volkstracht

IN THE MIDDLE AGES German country fashions were an imitation in rougher cloth of what the burgher was wearing in the towns. The high spirits and love of colour displayed at German festivals often came out in extravagant dress, and worthy rulers broke their heads on many occasions to suppress extravagance on such things as jewellery, gold, velvet and silk. One Saxon ordinance divided the population into five classes or *Stände* and prescribed exactly, and futilely, what the wives of each class might wear.

Then came the French Revolution, accompanied by romantic illusions about the peasant classes, and the ensuing revivals of local patriotism all over Europe. Encouraged and imitated by high fashion, the German countrymen stuck to the eighteenth-century version of their local dress, especially the more splendid styles appropriate to church-going, weddings and holidays.

One used to be able to trace a local costume right to the owner's village by looking at the detail, since the style never changed, and there were elaborate rules for what to wear and when. Married women had to cover their hair with a bonnet; unmarried girls at first wore wreaths (a myrtle wreath survives for weddings), but moved on to elaborate crowns and fan-shaped headdresses so

expensive that churches used to keep a stock of them for spinsters
to go to church in. The Altenburg crowns were so heavy that one
needed skill to balance them, and complaints were made that the
young women of Sankt Georg in the Black Forest wore crowns
which made them insufferably haughty.

The well-known leather shorts or breeches, braces with a
breastband, and white stockings only came into Bavaria from the
Tyrol after 1800, during the Wars of Liberation. If you want to
tell a Bavarian from a Tyrolese, look at the way he fastens his
leather breeches at the knee: Tyrolese breeches are buttoned,
while Bavarians wear a buckle; and only Tyrolese are supposed
to wear the broad belt, the *Bauchranze*, decorated with embroidery and brass rivets.

Nearly all the women's costumes include aprons. Red is a favourite colour; so is black, and not only for older women: Spree Forest girls engaged as nursemaids were still to be seen in Berlin in the 'twenties, wearing huge butterfly bows of black silk on the back of their heads. Frisian bodices blaze with silver ornaments. In the South, *dirndl* material sprigged with motifs of flowers, hearts or the heads of deer achieves great variety and creeps periodically into general summer fashion. Girls who do not fancy their skill at embroidery can go to the Tyrol and buy *Borten*, ribbons woven with intricate designs, for decoration.

Perhaps the most concentrated display of local costumes in the South German style can be found in Switzerland, at least for women; for men, the Tyrolese and Bavarian leather shorts and the small billycock hat with a bunch of chamois hair have taken a firm hold, and have been as much pirated by strangers as tartan in Scotland.

Folk-Dancing
Volkstanz

LOCAL DANCES in Germany have followed the folk-dancing pattern in most of Europe, vigorous rather than lyrical, and generally based on circles or lines. Sometimes there were games and masquerades, as in the woodcut by Nicholas Meldemann illustrating the 'Nose Dance' in which everyone wore a long artificial nose. Pair dancing arrived in the fourteenth century and survived in spite of head-shaking by the authorities. Last century the fashionable world stole the rustic *Ländler* and turned it into the 'rolling dance', the *Walzer*, which as the waltz has broken dramatically into fashionable dancing.

Northern Germany danced its *bunte Tänze*, eightsomes, four-somes, the 'Windmill' and the Schottische. On Rügen Island, in the *Schüddelbüx*, the man would pull up his sailor's trousers and dance a sort of hornpipe in front of his partner, while in Swabia they danced the *Kisseltanz*: the girl dances with a cushion in her hand and at the end of the dance kisses her partner as he kneels on it. You go on as often as you like with different partners.

The three-four time *Ländler* was modified into variants, none of which has raised such a dust as the *Schuhplattler* danced in Bavaria. First, to quiet music, the men dance with the girls, but at a given moment the couples glide apart and the girls merely spin round the edge of the floor, their skirts flying out so that they look like humming-tops, while the men leap, stamp and slap their knees, ankles and leather breeches in a deafening display of energy. It should be danced in the open, on a wooden stage like a boxing-ring, which magnifies the noise, to clarinettes, brass and accordions. The girls, always demure, are bare-headed in their neat plaits, but the true Bavarian man sticks to his billycock hat at all times.

Other Bavarian dances are performed to ballads, and in one, the couple hold fingers and turn their arms into patterns which tell the story.

Bringing the Cattle Home

Almabtrieb

FROM MID-OCTOBER onwards the cattle are brought down from the high Alpine pastures where they have grazed all summer. The herdsman and his wife get up early to tie decorations to the beasts' horns—coloured cloth, red ribbons, artificial flowers made of wood shavings, and bunches of feathers. The cows wear large copper bells slung round their necks on heavily decorated leather collars; the bells worn by the oxen are made of brass, smaller and higher in pitch, on simpler collars. A well-provided cattle-owner will possess thirty or forty cowbells, worth a great deal.

The cattle-owner drives his cart up to the pasture in the early morning, bringing the herdsman and his wife their Sunday clothes, and loads the cart with the simple furniture and utensils from the hut. The herd is rounded up and moves slowly on its long walk back to the village: the little herd-boys running ahead with the cows, followed by the calves, and last the oxen, with the herdsman and his wife walking behind.

Young and old turn out to see the cattle, and in the Pustertal the herdsman's wife throws *Schottenplatteln*—'Scottish biscuits' or oatcakes—to the children. People stop their cheering if a beast with black crape round its horns walks by. They know its owner has died in the summer.

Hunting Customs
Jagd

THE ART OF HUNTING in Germany (*Jagd* generally means what we understand by 'shooting') has always been beset by etiquette. The hunting colours are green, white and black. A boy used to be apprenticed to a master hunter for three years before he received the ritual box on the ear and was handed his hunting-knife 'not for idle use but for the wise and honourable purposes of this noble sport'. The precepts of hunting were learned by heart in preparation for a catechism couched in the form of riddles, and the jargon used is called *Jägerlatein*, 'huntsman's Latin'.

Huntsmen are superstitious. Ask a girl to jump over your gun, it will shoot all the straighter. Take an uneven number of cart-

ridges with you, preferably seven or more. Don't say 'Good luck' to a fellow-huntsman, say 'Break your neck and your leg as well' —*Hals und Beinbruch.*

Germans are fond of shooting with a dog, and all German sporting breeds are supposed to go back to dogs used by the Celts.

Shooting generally begins on St. Hubert's Day, November 3rd. It is strictly regulated and filled with ceremony, including the blowing of hunting-horns, formal greetings, a Court of Honour which can award fines in money for charity or rounds of drinks and a supper for the sportsmen (and their dogs) called a *Schüsseltreiben.*

There is next to no fox-hunting in Germany, but they have the advantage over us by preserving wild pig, which unlike the fox is eatable. German coverts are unfenced and generally unmarked, and keepers are unfriendly to loose dogs of any breed, so if you take a dog for a walk in a shooting district, keep him on a lead. Many keepers, like St. Hubert himself, grow tender-hearted towards the game. A few years ago I knew a young roebuck which had been taken home by the keeper when his mother was shot. The youngster was suckled by the keeper's bitch, and ran about the woods all day, known and respected by sportsmen, wearing a red collar. I visited the keeper one day when he was ill in bed; he summoned all his animals and fed them with bread in turn—the young roebuck, its foster-mother the bitch, a black-and-white cat, and a canary which sat patiently on the cat's head. After they had all had a piece, the keeper walked in his slippers through the kitchen into the stables to give the rest of the bread to his horse and two cows. The other animals followed us, politely but persistently, to see that there was fair play.

Martinmas

Sankt Martin

MARTIN is the patron Saint of geese because he is reported to have hidden among a flock of them in a stall, being too modest to want to be made Bishop of Tours. The geese raised a cackle and he was seized and crowned. In return for their service, geese are eaten at Martinmas.

Martin also gave half his cloak to a beggar, and the scene is enacted every year at a pageant in the Rhineland. It is difficult to chop one's own cloak in half with a sword while sitting on a horse, but the Saint manages it very neatly.

Lanterns come out at Martinmas, made of paper or pumpkins, and the children walk with them round the streets singing *Martinslieder;* and they make up rhymes asking for little presents called *Martinswecken.*

In Austria young men would go out on Martinmas Eve, masked and carrying pumpkin-lanterns on long poles, for a *Kasmanndl-fahrn*, shouting and making a great din with bells and the cracking of whips, for the benefit of evil spirits, who would thus be driven uphill into the empty herdsmen's huts on the high pastures until St. George's Day in April, when they would be driven out again.

Advent

GERMANS make an Advent Wreath out of sprigs of evergreen and fix four red candles in it. The wreath is stood on a table or hung from the ceiling, and the first candle is lit on the first Sunday after November 26th, the second and third on the following two Sundays, and the last on Christmas Eve. Children are given 'Advent calendars', and mark the days to Christmas by opening little windows, one each day; when your last window is open, it is Christmas.

Meanwhile St. Andrew's Night (*Andreasnacht*) comes along on 30th November. Young girls become curious about their future, and some wait up till midnight and then throw a slipper over their shoulder towards the door. If the toe of the slipper points outwards, a young man will come within a year and take the girl out of the house. If they want to know more about just which young man it is to be, they walk barefoot out of the house to a plum-tree, shake it and recite:

Tree, I shake thee,	*Bam, i schüttl di,*
Andrew, I pray thee	*Andre, i bitt di,*
Make a dog bark from	*lass mir a Hunderl bellen durt,*
Where my boy shall come.	*Wo mein Buab herkumma tuat.*

Advent was not a time to get married, but in the evenings one used to hear guns being fired and horns blown, to show that Christmas was coming. On St. Barbara's Day, 4th December, people would cut cherry-branches and put them in warm water near the stove so that they would bud in time for Christmas (in one district you had to go out dressed in nothing but a shirt and cut the branches with your back to the tree).

On St. Thomas' Eve, 21st December, the cook would bake the *Kletzenbrot*, a cake filled with dried pears (called *Kletzen*), plums, raisins, figs and nuts. Half-way through kneading the mixture she would go out into the orchard and embrace the fruit-trees to make them bear good fruit. It was a courting custom to give your young man the end off a *Kletzenbrot*.

St. Thomas' Night, the longest in the year, was called *Durchspinn-Nacht*, 'Spinning Night'. Sometimes girls would spin the night through to earn money for Christmas; or people would dance, play games, eat and drink to make the darkness shorter. Whatever Thomas thought about it himself, he brought apples and nuts to children in the Lüneburger Heide. And young girls could expect to dream of their future husbands if they got into bed on the wrong side and lay with their feet on the pillow.

Santa Claus

Nikolaus

SAINT NICHOLAS or Santa Claus or *Sünnerklas* brings German children presents on December 5th, accompanied by a servant variously called Knecht Ruprecht, Krampus or Hans Muff. Sometimes he calls in person, carrying a big book which is supposed to tell him all the things the children have been up to, and Ruprecht carries the presents and a birch for the naughty ones; sometimes he comes in the night, leaving presents, especially fruit, nuts and little biscuits, in the children's shoes, which in Friesland they leave by the fireplace as we do our stockings on Christmas Eve. In the South, the children find a *Klausemann*, a Santa Claus baked out of bread, on top of the pile.

Santa Claus has been put together from two saints, the Nicholas who was Bishop of Myra about the year 300, and Nicholas Bishop of Sion, who died in 564. Ruprecht comes from a pagan winter bogy. Our own Father Christmas in the red hooded jacket and the full white beard was first popular after Moritz von Schwind had drawn him.

The Knocking Nights
Klöpfelnächte

A KNOCKING NIGHT is the evening of one of the last three Thursdays before Christmas, when you collect your friends and move from house to house, knocking on the doors, throwing beans or small stones at the windows, and collecting the little presents which the long-suffering householders hand out to you. 'Knockers' are generally welcome, and in the Tyrol masked figures went with them; householders would ask the masked ones to jump about in the fields to make sure of a good harvest.

Another kind of 'knocker' would bang on the door, sing a brief song of praise to the owner of the house, and stick a pitchfork through the doorway. The householder was supposed to stick something nice to eat on the end of it.

You would also give presents on a 'knocking night', especially a little house made of sticks held together with blobs of dough, as a gift to your sweetheart. If she hangs it up from her ceiling, she loves you. And if you have a good friend, give him a present called a *Klöpfelscheit*, but throw it through his door and get away quickly. He will give you one in the same way on *Pfefferlestag*, 28th December.

Christmas

Weihnachten

WATCH NIGHT, *Weihnachten*, is associated with magical revelations. Mountains open and reveal their hoards of precious stones, church bells ring out from cities at the bottom of the sea, trees burst into blossom and fruit, the sun jumps thrice for joy, and the pure in heart can understand the language of animals.

Christmas has been celebrated on 25th December since the fourth century, but Christmas presents only date from the

Protestant fifteen-hundreds, when the Christ-child sent a bag of presents called a *Christbürde* to every German youngster. A proper 'Christmas load' contains five things: a toy, something nice to eat, a coin, something to wear, and a pencil-box, or what goes in it (called *Scholastika*). Later, everybody's presents were arranged on a table called a *Gabentisch*, and when the family gathered round it, this was the *Bescherung*, the 'giving'.

Christmas trees may have originated in Alsace. One was reported from Strasburg in 1604, decorated with paper roses, apples, little biscuits and pieces of sugar; and later Liselotte von der Pfalz wrote to her daughter from Northern France describing

'little box-trees with candles fastened to each branch', calling it 'a most pretty custom'. During the Wars of Liberation against Napoleon, Prussian officers imported the custom into Germany as far as Danzig, and Ludwig I's wife Therese introduced them into Bavaria. Christmas trees swept into Britain under Victoria and Albert and today look much the same in Germany and Britain, but Germans light theirs, find their presents underneath them, and embrace their relatives, on Christmas Eve (*Heiligabend*) instead of Christmas Day.

German citizens used to buy their Christmas presents at Christmas Markets. The markets at Berlin, Leipzig, Magdeburg, Frankfurt, Cologne and Nuremberg were famous throughout the country, and the Hamburg market was called the *Dom*, the cathedral, because it was set up in the precinct, while in Munich the *Kripperlmarkt* still specialises in Christmas cribs and carved figures to make up your own.

Some Germans eat carp on Christmas Eve, and many buy the long, loaf-shaped *Christstollen*, full of dried fruit and candied peel, which originated in Saxony and Thuringia. Spiced biscuits are another favourite, either shaped by hand or stamped out with elaborately-carved boxwood moulds: these are the Nuremberg *Lebkuchen*.

Like ourselves, Germans want to get the family together for Christmas and sit round their tree. They are very generous in giving presents, and '*Sie müder Weihnachtsmann*', 'you tired Father Christmas', is a good-natured nickname for someone moving very slowly, like the heavily-laden spirit of goodwill.

The Twelve Days of Christmas
Die Zwölf Rauhnächte

THE TWELVE DAYS were not always the same: in Bavaria and Austria they ran from Christmas Day to Epiphany; in Silesia they were the twelve days before Christmas, and in Franconia and Mecklenburg they started on New Year's Day. In any case, the air was heavy with magic. People near Siegen would not bake, roast or spin at this time; washing clothes was inadvisable in Bavaria. Monsters of all descriptions would swoop through the air, sometimes led by the 'wild hunter': headless beings, devil-swine and devil-hares, witches and sorcerers. The *getreue Eckart* with his staff and white beard would stride in front of this infernal army urging all humans to make way.

Many country people dressed up in devils' costumes to dance the fiends away. In the Tyrol the *Perchtenmasken* leaped about in the fields to make them fertile, or visited farmhouses, led by a man on a white horse, and danced to music until a 'witch' came with a broom and swept them out.

A girl could tell her own fortune in the Twelve Days by throwing her slipper twelve times into a pear-tree: if it stuck once in the tree, she would marry her heart's desire.

New Year's Eve
Silvester

IN 1494 SEBASTIAN BRANT wrote in his *Narrenschiff*, the 'Vessel of Fools', that New Year was the time for 'casting bullets, cutting rods for water-divining, burying treasure and similar matters', and a German New Year's Eve party is still not complete without a game of *Bleigiessen*—pouring molten lead from a ladle into a bowl of water and telling fortunes from the shapes into which the lead hardens.

In Germany 'the clock strikes thirteen' and there is general and noisy rejoicing. Village night-watchmen would climb the church tower and 'blow the New Year in' with horns. Some householders left a door open for the Old Year to go out, and a shutter for the New Year to come in by, Bavarians would put out the light just before twelve and light it again when midnight struck, and along the Weser the village lads would carry a straw doll through the village, throw it into the river and come back with a pretty girl, their New Year's Queen. Silesians would drink from a loving-cup and throw it out of the window, and in Saxony they would jump on chairs and tables at the first stroke of midnight and jump down at the last, shouting '*Grüss dich Gott, du neues Jahr!*' And along the Rhine, they sing.

Young people in the Alps still love to get outside and make loud noises, cracking whips, letting off shotguns and even firing blanks from baby cannon called *Böller*. Older people stay in and drink punch, and some still forecast the weather for the coming year with an 'onion calendar', a *Zwiebelkalender*. Cut an onion into twelve slices and lay them in a row, one for each month, sprinkle them with salt and watch which slice weeps the most juice: that will be the rainiest.

If the first person you meet on New Year's Day is a small boy, he will bring you luck.

Epiphany
Drei König

AFTER THE RELICS of the Three Wise Kings were brought to Cologne from Milan in the twelfth century there were many miracle plays about Gaspar, Melchior and Balthasar and their journey to Bethlehem, first in churches and then, with great splendour, in the open. The dark-skinned Gaspar generally had the comic lines, and in the course of centuries the name Kaspar became *Kasperle*, the hero of the German Punch-and-Judy show.

The Reformation killed miracle plays about the Three Kings, but 'Star Singers', *Sternsinger*, wearing golden crowns and carrying a star on a long staff, still walk the streets. In Saxony the children carried a little house inside the star, with Herod looking out of it, and in the Harz, children from poor mountain villages had a traditional right to be *Sterngucker*, 'star seekers', and to expect presents.

This was the time to take salt, especially rock-salt for cattle, and chalk to be blessed in church. Put the salt into the mangers and the cattle will thrive. When you get home, write the initials of the three Wise Kings—K for Kaspar, M for Melchior, B for Balthasar—on your door with the chalk, add crosses and the date, and you will stay lucky the whole year through.

Water-diviners would cut their hazel rods on 6th January and dedicate them to Kaspar for seeking gold, to Melchior for water, and to Balthasar for silver.

Fasting Eve

Fastnacht (South Germany); *Fasnacht* (Switzerland); *Fasching* (Bavaria); *Karneval* (Cologne, Rhineland and Mainz)

THE COMPLICATED RITUALS of dancing in fancy dress, marching through the streets, and ridiculing the authorities in songs and huge three-dimensional caricatures carried on floats, begin at 11 minutes past 11 on the 11th of November and last until Ash Wednesday, except in Basel, which drums its way through three days and nights of noisy freedom starting the Monday after Lent has begun. The societies, which celebrate first by themselves and then parade the streets, organise evenings at which, in the Rhineland for instance, a *Büttenredner* is hauled up to the roof-beams in a barrel and extemporises wit at the expense of one and all. In Bonn the *Stadtsoldaten*, the City Soldiers, march in blue-and-white eighteenth-century uniforms, well provided with clay pipes, soup-spoons and a field kitchen called a *Goulaschkanone*, while in Basel over a hundred 'Companies' thunder round the narrow streets armed with kettle-drums, all dressed alike—as toothpaste-tubes, ducks or witches according to this year's fancy. A Prince Carnival appears, splendidly dressed, with his Princess, and squads of girls in shakos, hussars' jackets, short skirts and boots (the origin of American drum-majorettes) dance high-kicks in the cold as the crowd link arms, sway and sing. The Rhineland keeps fit on wine and Munich says it with beer. It is the great occasion in the year for townsmen to let themselves go, and comes down from fourteenth-century apprentices and their love of public dancing and marching and showing impertinence to the authorities.

In the Alpine villages men still dance in heavy wooden masks or in grotesque costumes of feathers and straw twice the height of a man, sometimes swinging cowbells. At Aussee in the Steiermark masked figures called *Flinserln* march behind masked musicians on Shrove Tuesday, men and women in pairs, in tall pointed hats. The hats are gilt and the marchers' clothes are sewn with hundreds of gold and silver scales which glitter in the sun. The masked figures sing a song called *Faschingstag* in a high falsetto and reward children who sing loudly with nuts, which they carry in white bags.

The fantastic wooden masks which used to dance the fields have mainly gone into the folk museums, but the energy with which German citizens enjoy themselves and spend their money at this time of year survives in the tradition, at Munich, that you go to

the fountain on Ash Wednesday and wash out your empty purse.

Lent has come, but the guilds will still be celebrating on Ash Wednesday, and on the first Sunday in Lent, *Funkensonntag* or 'Spark Sunday', flaming wheels and bonfires will be kissing Carnival good-bye, and the year will take a brief rest until the German love of noise, decoration, colour and ritual erupts in the Spring festivals.

Notes on Some Illustrations

p. 36   Jesus washing the disciples' feet. Hermann Bungert, fifteenth century.

p. 37   Jesus carrying the cross. Hermann Bungert, fifteenth century.

p. 38   The Resurrection. Hermann Bungert, fifteenth century.

p. 39   Easter Eggs from Mardorf, Hessen. From Erich Meyer-Heysig's *Deutsche Volkskunst*, published by Prestel Verlag, Munich.

p. 42   The Witches, by Albrecht Dürer, after Hans Baldung Grien. Baldung's monogram on the tablet has been replaced by Dürer's initials.

p. 44   Woodcut from the *Schedelsche Weltchronik*, printed by Anton Koberger at Nuremberg, 1493.

p. 46   Ascension Day. Woodcut. *Germanisches National-Museum*, Nuremberg.

p. 48   Design for a shooting target by Moritz von Schwind.

p. 49   The 'Bird Meadow' at Dresden in the year 1612. *Germanisches National-Museum*, Nuremberg.

p. 51   Upper panel of a cupboard painted by Bartholomäus Lämmler in 1836. From Rudolph Hanhart's *Appenzeller Bauernmalerei*, published by Verlag Arthur Niggli, Teufen.

p. 52   Bridal waggon loaded for a farm wedding in the Egerland. Lithograph, about 1820. *Germanisches National-Museum*, Nuremberg.

pp. 54, 55   Farm wedding in the Egerland. *Germanisches National-Museum*, Nuremberg.

pp. 56, 57, 58   Silhouettes from the *Münchner Bilderbogen*, Munich.

p. 59   Decorated card announcing the birth of a daughter to Herr Bock, a dentist, at Nuremberg in 1879. *Germanisches National-Museum*, Nuremberg.

p. 62   Lutheran christening at Augsburg, early eighteenth century. *Germanisches National-Museum*, Nuremberg.

p. 64   Woodcut by J. Koelhoff the Younger from the *Chronik von Köln*, 1499.

pp. 65, 66   A Corpus Christi sampler worked by Maria Brunner in 1852.

p. 67   The Fishermen's Jousting-Match at Ulm on 10th August 1818. Copperplate engraving. *Stadtarchiv*, Ulm.

p. 69   The Oberammergau stage in 1840.

p. 72   Peasants dancing under a lime-tree. Woodcut by D. Kandel from H. Bock's *Kräuterbuch*, printed at Strasburg in 1546.

p. 73   The Shepherd's Race at Markgröningen in 1862. *Germanisches National-Museum*, Nuremberg.

pp. 75, 76   From *Destillierkunst* (*The Art of Distilling*) by Hieronymus Brunschwig, printed at Strasburg by Johann Grüninger in 1500. Taken from Albert Schramm's *Der Bilderschmuck der Frühdrücke*, published at Leipzig, 1921–1943.

p. 77   Lower panel of a cupboard painted by Conrad Starck, from Rudolf Hanhart's *Appenzeller Bauernmalerei*, published by Verlag Arthur Niggli, Teufen.

p. 78   Hop-picking near Straubing. *Bayrisches Nationalmuseum*, Munich.

p. 80   Figure of St. Michael by Stefan Vögner from the Lower Inn valley. *Ferdinandeum*, Innsbruck.

p. 83   Harvest, by Ludwig Richter. *Staatliche Graphische Sammlung*, Munich.

pp. 84, 85   Silhouettes from the *Münchner Bilderbogen*. *Germanisches National-Museum*, Nuremberg.

p. 87   The first October Fair at Munich in 1810. *Stadtmuseum*, Munich.

p. 88   Silhouette from the *Münchner Bilderbogen*. *Germanisches National-Museum*, Nuremberg.

p. 89   A Swabian vineyard about 1700. *Germanisches National-Museum*, Nuremberg.